Math Analogies

BEGINNING

Math Analogies products available in print, software, or eBook form.

Beginning • Level 1 • Level 2
Level 3 • Level 4

Written by
Linda Brumbaugh
Doug Brumbaugh

Graphic Design by
Trisha Dreyer
Karla Garrett
Annette Langenstein

© 2009
THE CRITICAL THINKING CO.™
www.CriticalThinking.com
Phone: 800-458-4849 • Fax: 541-756-1758
1991 Sherman Ave., Suite 200 • North Bend • OR 97459
ISBN 978-1-60144-196-6

Reproduction of This Copyrighted Material
The intellectual material in this product is the copyrighted property of The Critical Thinking Co.™ The individual or entity who initially purchased this product from The Critical Thinking Co.™ or one of its authorized resellers is licensed to reproduce (print or duplicate on paper) each page of this product for use within one home or one classroom. Our copyright and this limited reproduction permission (user) agreement strictly prohibit the sale of any of the copyrighted material in this product. Any reproduction beyond these expressed limits is strictly prohibited without the written permission of The Critical Thinking Co.™ Please visit http://www.criticalthinking.com/copyright for more information. The Critical Thinking Co.™ retains full intellectual property rights on all its products (eBooks, books, and software).
Printed in the United States of America by McNaughton & Gunn, Inc., Saline, MI (Jan. 2019)

Teaching Suggestions

Analogies occur in life and frequently in high-stakes tests. Understanding analogies and the ability to reason analogically (reasoning used to identify, evaluate, and solve an analogy) are also important problem-solving skills. It is, therefore, beneficial for students to learn about analogies as soon as reasonably possible.

The immediate benefit is to recognize and solve simple analogies. The long-term benefits are improved reasoning skills that enable students to break problems into their component parts, recognize analogies embedded in arguments, and evaluate them.

Problem-solving is an essential part of mathematical development. Analogies provide practice in breaking math problems down into their component parts, making it easier to recognize familiar formats that enable students to produce solutions.

Analogical reasoning is not easy, particularly for younger students whose thinking skills are in the formative stages of development. At this age, children commonly use guesswork instead of organized analysis to solve problems. For example, ask young children for two numbers between 10 and 15 and they will often guess or start counting from 1 to find the answer.

A challenge for young students learning to solve analogies is reading the format. For example, "A : a :: B : " is read "A is to a as B is to." This is not common language for a youngster. The interpretation skills mandate the realization that the phrase "is to" implies a connection between the item to the left and right of the phrase. Then, the word "as" relays the idea that there is a similar connection between the next two items, only one of which is provided.

On pages iv and v, we provide introductory lessons to help students read and understand analogies. We encourage teachers to work one-on-one with K-1 students through this lesson, and then monitor student work until it is clear the student grasps the meaning of an analogy.

We recommend that students draw and verbalize their answers. The drawing develops fine motor skills and the verbalization develops communication skills. Some young children may find drawing answers too challenging, but might be able to verbalize solutions. At this age, that is fine. However, these children should be encouraged to attempt to draw the solution after they verbalize it. Remember to keep learning fun.

The beauty of many of the items presented here is that they are language independent. Thus, non-native English-speaking students have the opportunity to participate with all other students in the challenges presented. When all students are involved, each one has the opportunity to learn the basics and beauty of logic and mathematics while developing and strengthening language skills.

The National Council of Teachers of Mathematics defined five content strands that should appear in the K-12 mathematics curriculum. These five strands are:

- Number and Operations
- Algebra
- Geometry
- Measurement
- Data Analysis and Probability

The entries in this book are built around grade-appropriate standards for each of those five strands. While some of the analogies may appear too difficult or too easy for a student, there will be other related entries that should be suitable. If the analogies in this book become too easy for the student, try the next level, which is more challenging.

"Remember to keep learning fun."

Table of Contents

INTRODUCTION
Teaching Suggestions ii
Sample Lessons .... iv-v
About the Authors vi

EXERCISES 1-38

NCTM Standards (National Council of Teachers of Mathematics)

Number and Operations	1, 4, 7, 12, 15, 17, 23, 26, 30, 32, 34, 37, 39, 44, 46, 50, 52, 55, 56, 58, 60, 63, 65, 67, 70, 74, 76, 81, 83, 86, 92, 98, 102, 106, 110, 114, 118, 122, 126, 129, 132, 135, 139, 143, 146, 149
Algebra	2, 3, 5, 8, 13, 16, 18, 22, 24, 27, 31, 33, 35, 38, 40, 45, 47, 51, 53, 57, 59, 61, 66, 68, 71, 75, 77, 82, 84, 87, 89, 91, 93, 95, 97, 99, 101, 103, 105, 107, 109, 111, 113, 115, 117, 119, 121, 123, 125, 127, 130, 133, 136, 140, 145, 147, 150
Geometry	6, 9, 10, 14, 19, 25, 28, 36, 41, 48, 54, 62, 69, 72, 78, 85, 88, 94, 104, 108, 112, 120, 128, 131, 141, 144, 148
Measurement	11, 20, 21, 29, 42, 49, 64, 73, 79, 90, 96, 116, 124, 134, 138, 142, 145, 151
Data Analysis and Probability	43, 80, 100, 137, 152

ANSWERS 39

Math Analogy Sample Lessons

Teacher:

"The first girl is smiling. The second girl is frowning."

"To make these boys match the girls, what should the second boy look like?"

Teacher:

"This circle is white."

"This circle is black."

"To make the squares match the circles, what do we have to do to this square?"

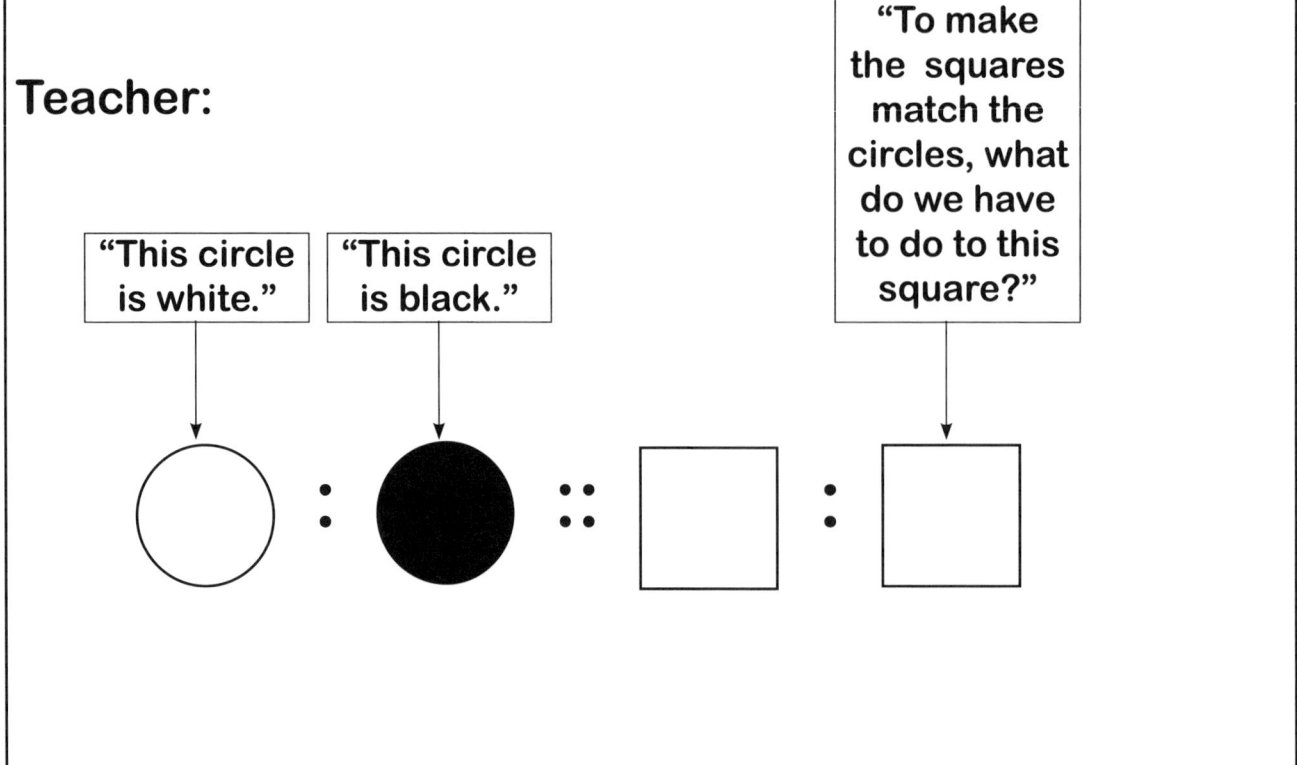

Math Analogies Beginning

Sample Lessons

Teacher:

"This boy is pointing up." "This boy is pointing down."

"To make the arrows match the boys, where should the next arrow point, up or down?"

  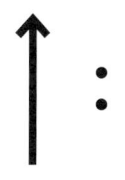

Teacher:

"The first girl is big. The second girl is small."

"To make the two circles match the two girls, what should the next circle look like?"

  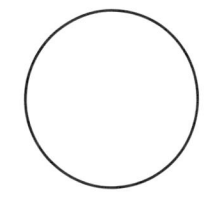

About the Authors

Linda S. Brumbaugh

I retired after teaching a total of 31 years in grades three, four, and five. Both my BS from the University of Florida and Masters from the University of Central Florida are in Elementary Education. As I look back over my teaching career, I enjoyed seeing the excitement on the children's faces as they encountered new concepts, worked with a manipulative, experienced some new mathematical application, or played a new mathematical game. It was stimulating when they solved an intricate problem, discovered something new to them, or got caught up in some new mathematical trick. As they got excited about learning, so did I. Each day of every year brought some new learning opportunity for me and for the children. I continue to work with pre-school and elementary-age children in the Sunday school system of our church. Our intent is to convey some of that excitement to each child who uses this book.

Douglas K. Brumbaugh

I taught close to 50 years before retiring after 35 years at the University of Central Florida. I taught in a variety of settings: college, in-service and almost daily in a K-12 setting. I received my BS from Adrian College and my Masters and Doctorate in Mathematics Education at the University of Georgia. Students change, classroom environments change, the curriculum changes, and I change. The thoughts and examples used here are based on my teaching experiences over the years. Our hope is that the thoughts in this book will spark the mathematical interest of each child who works with them.

Math Analogies Beginning

Complete Each Math Analogy

1)

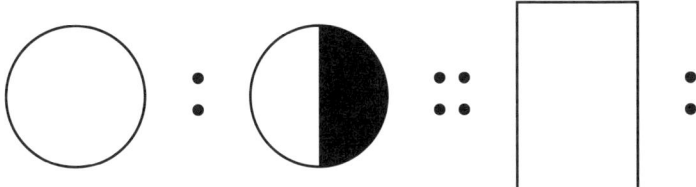

2)

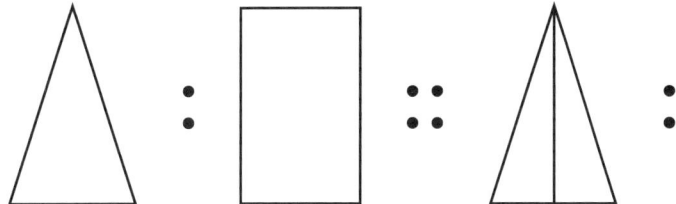

3)

4)

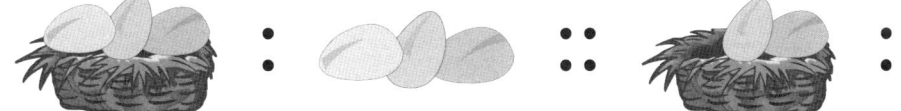

Math Analogies Beginning

Complete Each Math Analogy

5)
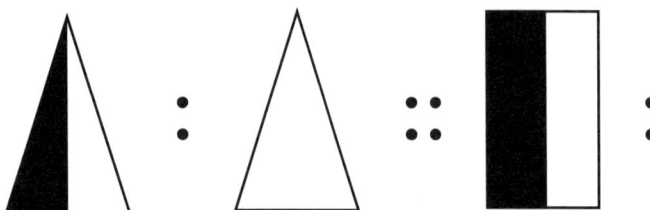

6)
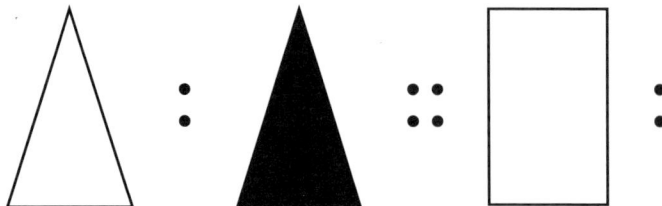

7)

two : **2** :: three :

8)
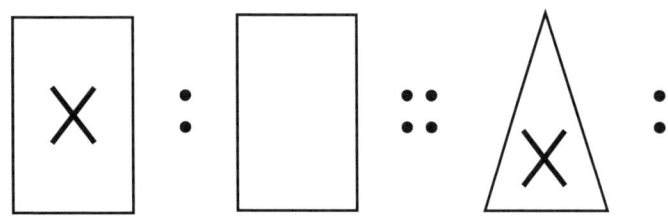

Complete Each Math Analogy

9) ○ : Ⓧ :: ▭ :

10) ○—○ : ○— :: □—□ :

11) ruler : length :: scale :

12) one : 1 :: two :

Complete Each Math Analogy

13)

14)
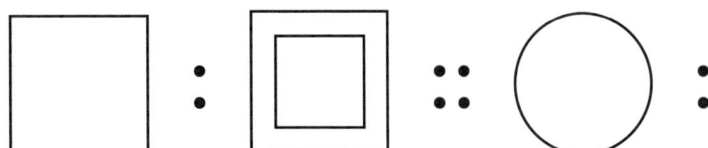

15)

16)
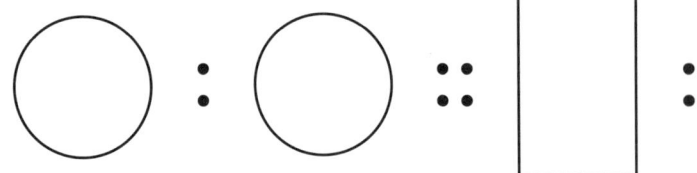

Complete Each Math Analogy

17)

18)

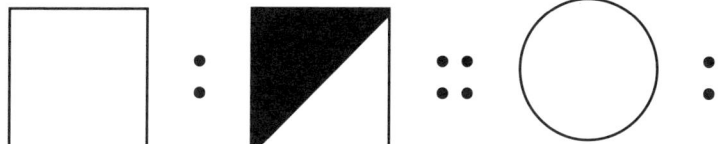

19)

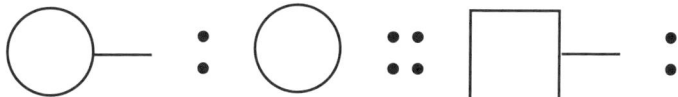

20)

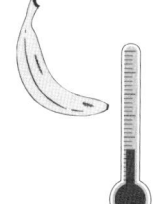 : cold ::  :

Complete Each Math Analogy

21)

22)

23)

24)

Complete Each Math Analogy

25)

26)

27)

X : x :: **O** :

28)

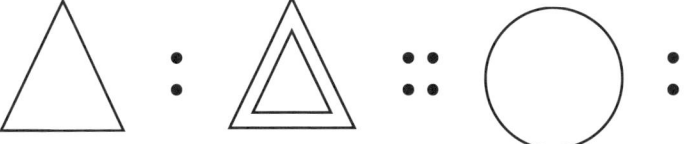

Complete Each Math Analogy

29) full : [pitcher] :: empty :

30) two : ●● :: three :

31) xX : X :: oO :

32) ⬅ : ➡ :: ◁ :

Complete Each Math Analogy

33)

 : ☐ :: 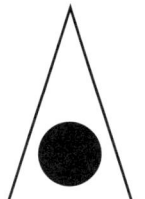 :

34)

 : one ::  :

35)

 : 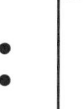 :: :

36)

 :  ::  :

Complete Each Math Analogy

37)

three : ◯◯◯ :: two :

38)

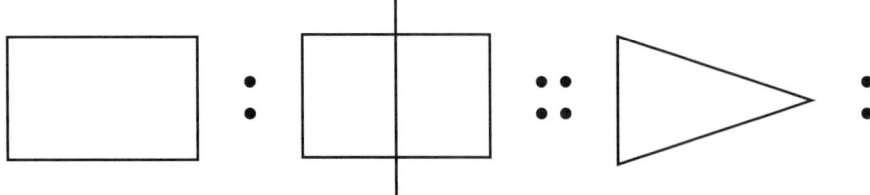

39)

40)

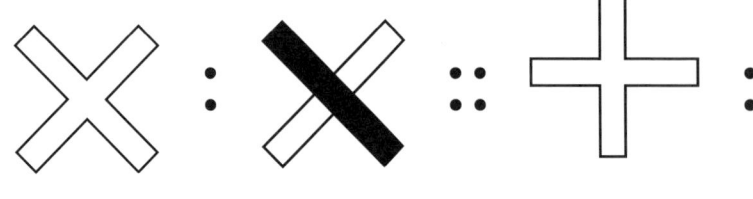

Math Analogies Beginning   Exercises

Complete Each Math Analogy

41)

42)

 : 5 ::  :

43)

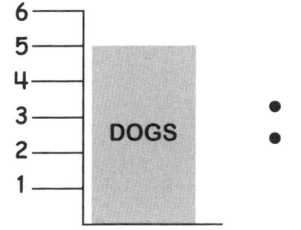 : 5 dogs :: 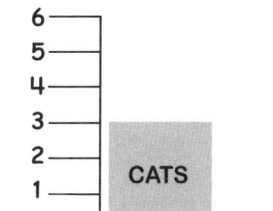 :

44)

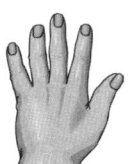 : 5 ::  :

© 2009 The Critical Thinking Co.™ • www.CriticalThinking.com • 800-458-4849   11

Math Analogies Beginning   Exercises

Complete Each Math Analogy

45) ○ : ◯▲ :: □ :

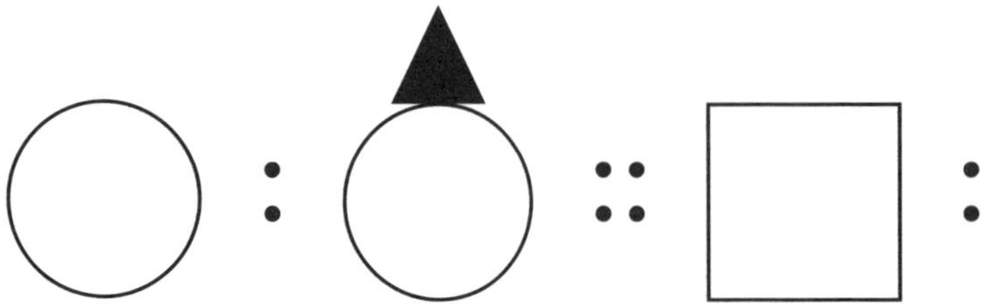

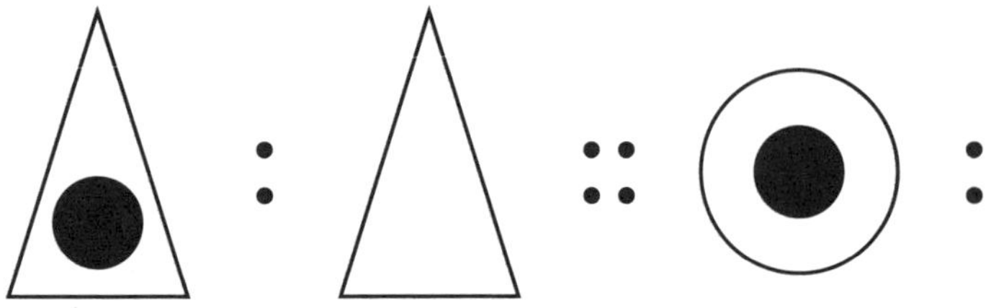

46) Ⓘ Ⓘ (two lines in circle) : Ⓘ Ⓘ Ⓘ (three lines in circle) :: ▯ ▯ (two lines in square) :

47) △• (triangle with dot) : △ :: ⊙ (circle with dot) :

48) L (outline) : L (filled) :: T (outline) :

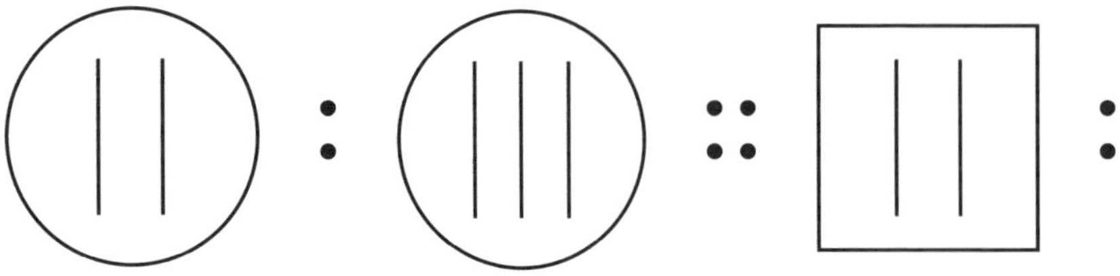

Complete Each Math Analogy

49)

day : week :: week :

50)

 : :: 2 :

51)

U : ∩ :: W :

52)

 : 4 :: :

Math Analogies Beginning · Exercises

Complete Each Math Analogy

53)

54)

55)

 : 6¢ ::  :

56)

Math Analogies Beginning — Exercises

Complete Each Math Analogy

57) 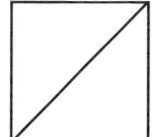 : 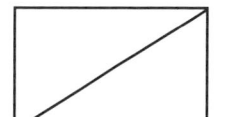 :: [rectangle with diagonal] :

58) 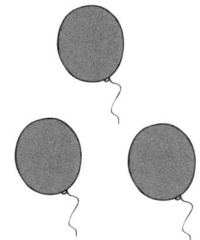 : 3 :: 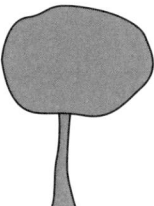  :

59) Y : y :: X :

60)  :  :: ◯ :

Complete Each Math Analogy

61) ▢ : ▫ :: ◯ :

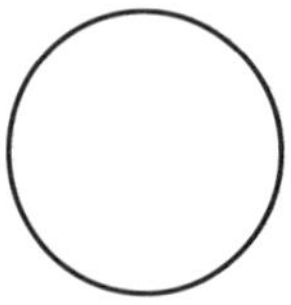

62) ♡ : ♡ :: ◯ :

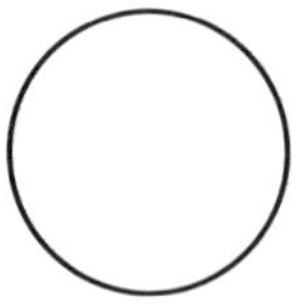

63) triangle left : △ | :: circle right :

64) ✏ 3¢ : ✏✏ 6¢ :: 🍎 5¢ :

Math Analogies Beginning

Complete Each Math Analogy

65)

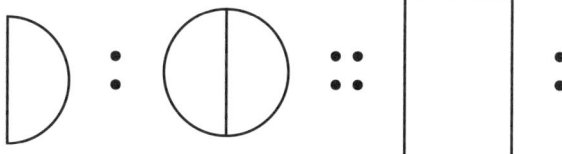

66)

67)

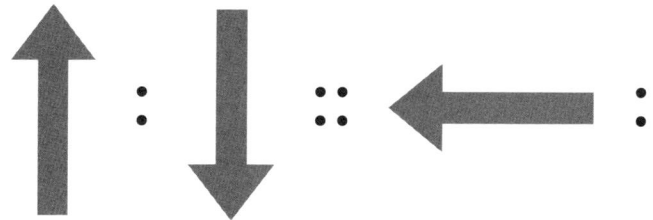

68)

Complete Each Math Analogy

69)

Y : ⅄ :: T :

70)

✩✩✩✩ : 4 :: 🍓🍓🍓🍓🍓 :

71)

e : ǝ :: p :

72)

⬆️(circle) : ⬇️(circle) :: ⬇️(square) :

Math Analogies Beginning Exercises

Complete Each Math Analogy

73)

 : **10¢** ::  :

74)

 : **5** :: 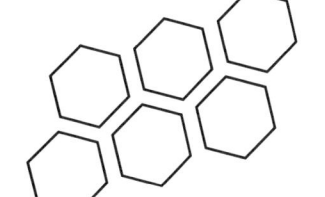 :

75)

 :  ::

76)

 :  ::

Complete Each Math Analogy

77)

p : q :: d :

78)

Y⅄ : ⅄Y :: T⊥ :

79)

minutes : hours :: day :

80)

 : no rain ::  :

Complete Each Math Analogy

81)

big : little :: **tall** :

82)

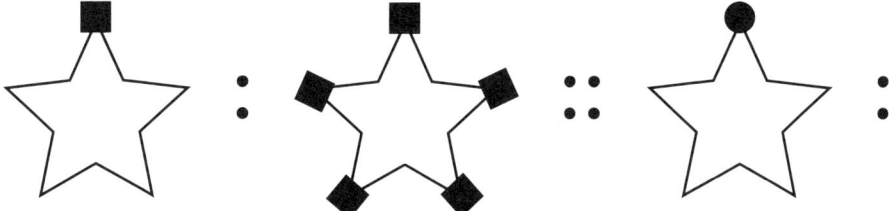

83)

3 : 4 :: 1 :

84)

Σ : Ƹ :: > :

Complete Each Math Analogy

85)

← : ↔ :: ⊢ :

86)

first : second :: second :

87)

🌳 : 🌳 :: 🎂 :

88)

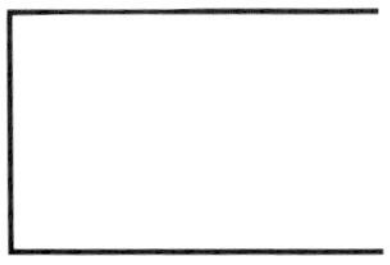

▭ : ▭ :: ▭ :

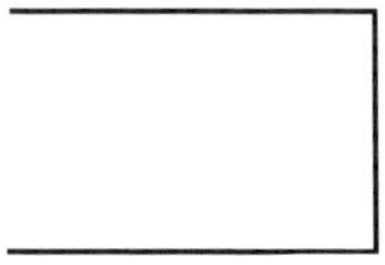

Math Analogies Beginning

Complete Each Math Analogy

89)

90)

91)
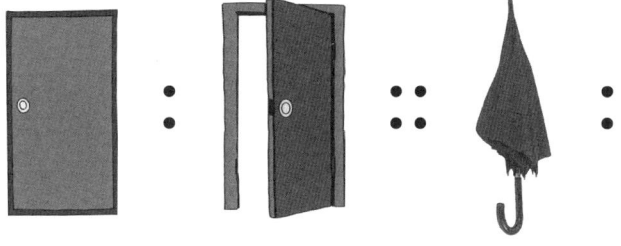

92)

Complete Each Math Analogy

93)

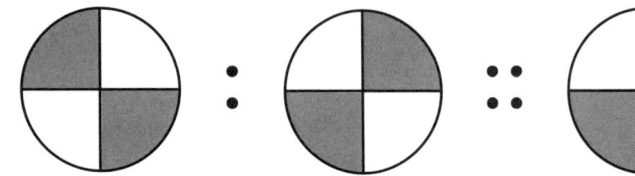

94)

circle : ◯ :: triangle :

95)

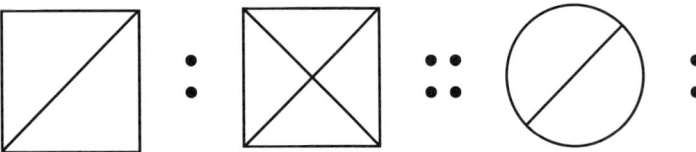

96)

Complete Each Math Analogy

97)

 : 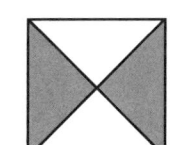 ::  :

98)

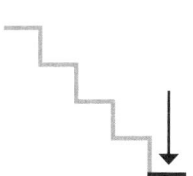 : bottom :: 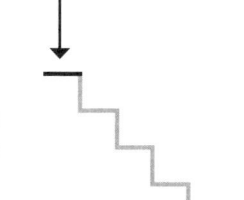 :

99)

 :   ::  :

100)

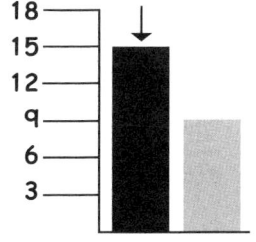 : more :: 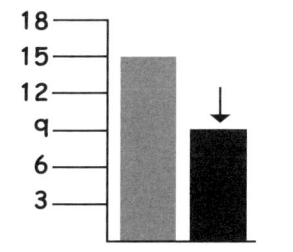 :

Math Analogies Beginning

Complete Each Math Analogy

101)

102)

103)

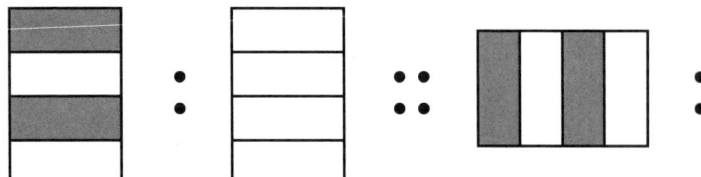

104)

circle : ◯ :: square :

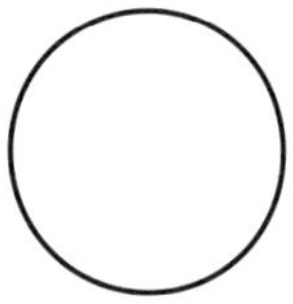

Complete Each Math Analogy

105)

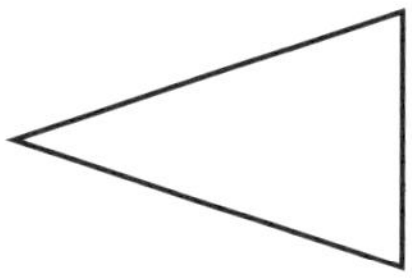

◁ : ▷ :: ▽ :

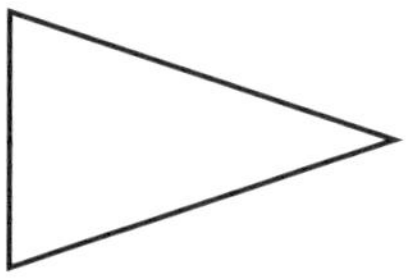

106)

above the bar : 𝄞 :: below the bar :

107)

S : s :: Z :

108)

square : □ :: rectangle :

Complete Each Math Analogy

109)

| : + :: ✳ :

110)

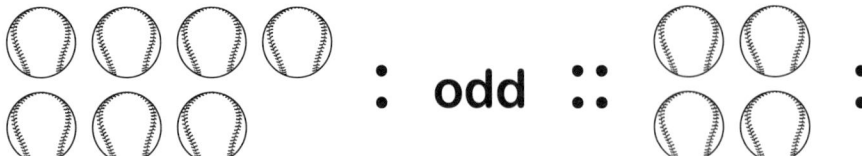

8 baseballs : odd :: 5 baseballs :

111)

○○ : ○○○ :: ○○○○ :

112)

die(3) : 3 :: die(5) :

Complete Each Math Analogy

113)

OX : XO :: LM :

114)

eight : 8 :: ten :

115)

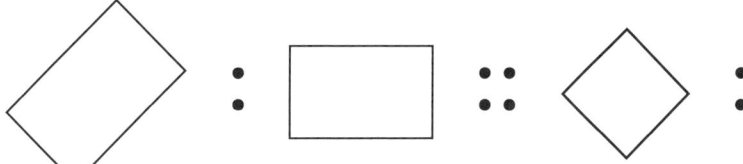

116)

 : 1:30 ::  :

Complete Each Math Analogy

117)

add : **+** :: subtract :

118)

seven : **7** :: six :

119)

red : r :: blue :

120)

triangle : △ :: circle :

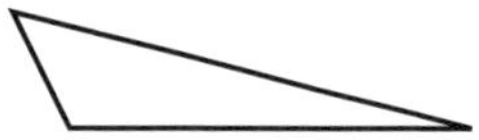

Math Analogies Beginning

Complete Each Math Analogy

121)

g : girl :: b :

122)

four : 4 :: nine :

123)

○○○ : ●○○● :: ○○○○ :

124)

 : 3¢ ::  :

Complete Each Math Analogy

125)

2 : 3 :: 4 :

126)

quarter : 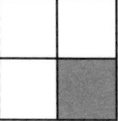 :: half :

127)

5 : 4 :: 3 :

128)

left : ⬅ :: right :

Math Analogies Beginning

Complete Each Math Analogy

129)

half : 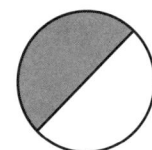 :: quarter : _____

130)

six : 7 :: eight : _____

131)

symmetric : 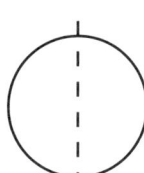 :: not symmetric : _____

132)

fourth : 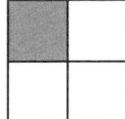 :: half : _____

Complete Each Math Analogy

133)

mail : **m** :: tail :

134)

12 inches : foot :: **3** feet :

135)

third : ⬤ :: quarter :

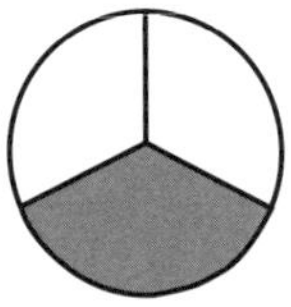

136)

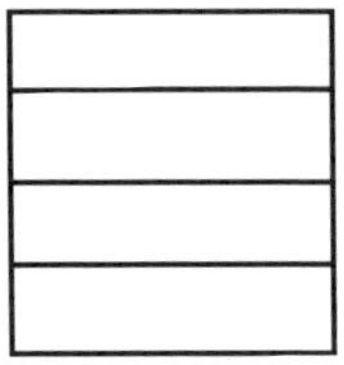

▯ : ▯ :: ▯ :

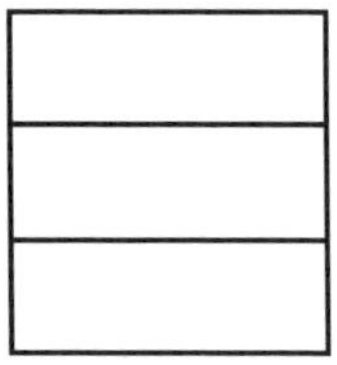

Complete Each Math Analogy

137)

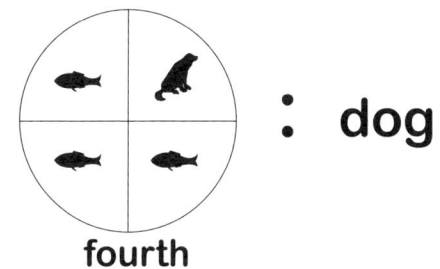 : dog :: 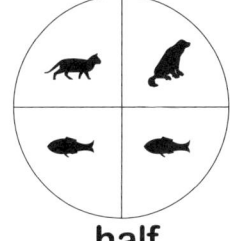 :

fourth   half

138)

ounce : light :: ton :

139)

3 + 5 : 8 :: 8 - 5 :

140)

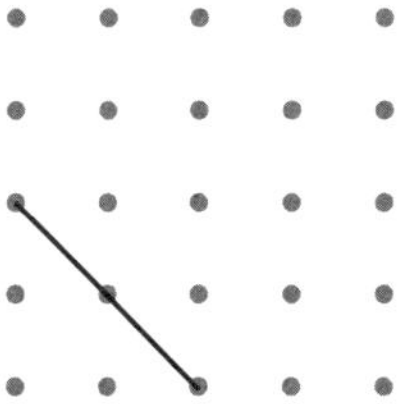

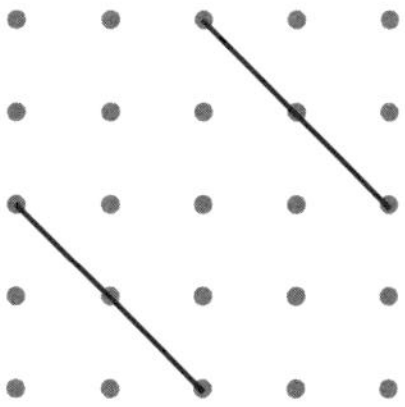

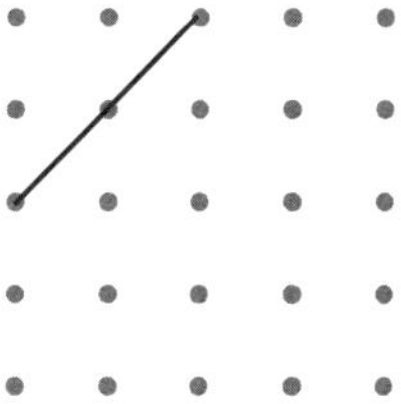

Math Analogies Beginning — Exercises

Complete Each Math Analogy

141)

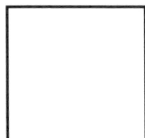 : **4** sides ::  :

142)

many :  :: few :

143)

 : even ::  :

144)

3 corners :  :: **4** corners :

Complete Each Math Analogy

145)

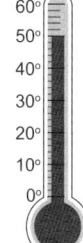 : **50°** :: 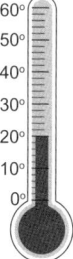 :

146)

 : tall ::  :

147)

 : :: :

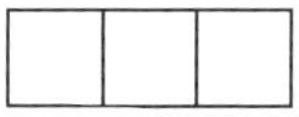

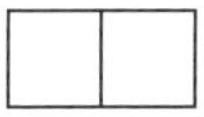

148)

 :  ::  :

symmetric   not symmetric

Complete Each Math Analogy

149)

A : a :: B :

150)

hot : h :: cold :

151)

 : 5¢ ::  :

152)

Sunday : Tuesday :: Saturday :

Answers

Sample Lessons

iv)

iv)

v)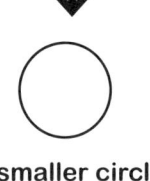

v) (smaller circle)

Page 1

1)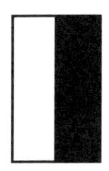

2)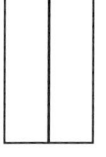

3)

4)

Page 2

5)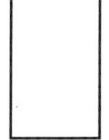

6)

7) 3

8)

Page 3

9)

10)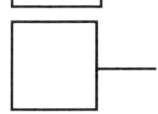

11) weight

12) 2

Page 4

13)

14)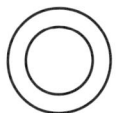

15) 2

16)

Page 5

17)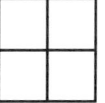

18)

19)

20) hot

Page 6

21)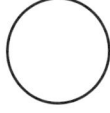

22)

23)

24)

Page 7

25)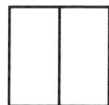

26) 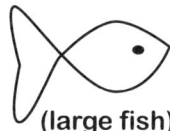 (large fish)

27) O (small o)

28)

Page 8

29)

Math Analogies Beginning — Answers

30) (3 black circles)
31) O (big O)
32) ▷

Page 9
33) △
34) two
35) ○ (big circle)
36) (circle half black)

Page 10
37) ○ ○
38) ▷ (with vertical line)
39) two
40) (plus sign, horizontal bar white, vertical bar black)

Page 11
41) (square, top white, bottom black)
42) 1

43) 3 cats
44) 5

Page 12
45) (square with black triangle on top)
46) (square with 3 vertical lines)
47) ○
48) T

Page 13
49) month
50) 1
51) M
52) 3

Page 14
53) (circle with black dot inside)
54) ▷
55) 7¢
56) (gray balloon)

Page 15
57) (rectangle with X)
58) 2
59) x (small x)
60) (circle with vertical line through middle)

Page 16
61) ○ (smaller circle)
62) (circle within circle)
63) | ○
64) (two apples) 10¢

Page 17
65) (rectangle divided in half vertically)
66) (heart, left white, right black)
67) → (gray arrow)
68) ▷

Math Analogies Beginning — Answers

Page 18

69) ⊥
70) 5
71) d
72) ↑ (in box)

Page 19

73) 10¢
74) 6
75) □
76)

Page 20

77) b
78) ⊥T
79) week
80) rain

Page 21

81) short
82)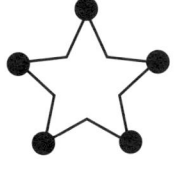

83) 2
84) <

Page 22

85) ⊢⊣
86) third
87)
88) ⌒

Page 23

89) ○
90) 4:15
91)
92) third or last

Page 24

93)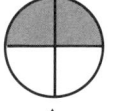
94)
95)
96) 4:30

Page 25

97)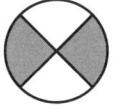
98) top
99)
100) less

Page 26

101)
102) 4
103)
104)

Page 27

105)
106)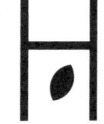
107) z (small z)
108)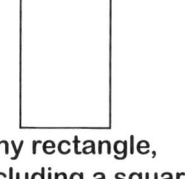

(any rectangle, including a square is acceptable)

Page 28

109)

Math Analogies Beginning — Answers

110) even
111) ◯◯◯◯◯
112) 4

Page 29

113) ML
114) 10
115) ◻
116) 5:45

Page 30

117) -
118) 6
119) b
120) ◯

Page 31

121) boy
122) 9
123) ●◯◯◯●
124) 7¢

Page 32

125) 5

126)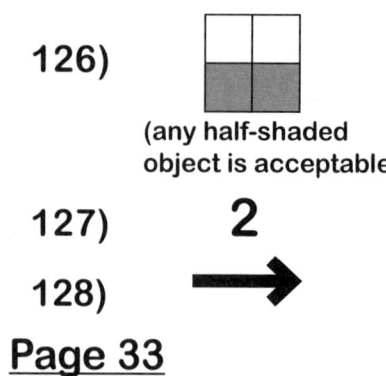
(any half-shaded object is acceptable)

127) 2
128) ➜

Page 33

129) (any quarter-shaded object is acceptable)

130) 9

131) (any non-symmetric object is acceptable)

132)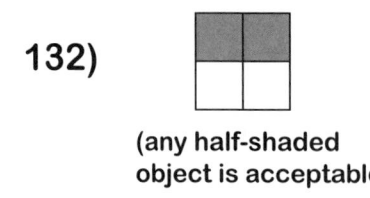
(any half-shaded object is acceptable)

Page 34

133) t
134) yard
135) (any quarter-shaded object is acceptable)

136) ◻

Page 35

137) fish

138) heavy
139) 3
140)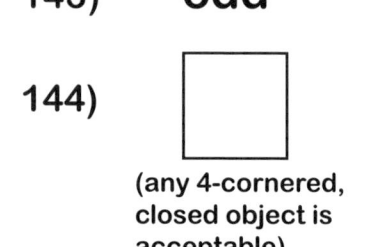

Page 36

141) 3 sides
142) ◯◯ (any number of circles less then 5 is acceptable)
143) odd
144) ◻ (any 4-cornered, closed object is acceptable)

Page 37

145) 20°
146) short
147) ◻
148) ◯ (any non-symmetric circle is acceptable)

Page 38

149) b
150) c
151) 3¢
152) Monday